CAREY PRICE

BY TODD KORTEMEIER

PRESS BOX
BOOKS

Press Box Books is an imprint of Press Room Editions.

This book is distributed exclusively in Canada by Saunders Book Company, PO Box 308, Collingwood ON L9Y 3Z7. For sales information, call 800-461-9120, or email info@saundersbook.ca. **www.saundersbook.ca**

Produced for Press Box Books by Red Line Editorial.

Photographs ©: Matt Slocum/AP Images, cover, 1, 30; Jacques Boissinot/AP Images, 5, 6; Chris Harris/All Canada Photos/Corbis, 9; Alistair Scott/Shutterstock Images, 10; Richard Lam/AP Images, 12–13; Anders Wiklund/Scanpix/AP Images, 14; Bradley C. Bower/AP Images, 17; Darryl Dyck/The Canadian Press/AP Images, 18; Mark Humphrey/AP Images, 21, 23; Eric Canha/Cal Sport Media/AP Images, 25; Philippe Bouchard/Cal Sport Media/AP Images, 26; Red Line Editorial/bergserg/Shutterstock Images, 29

ISBN
978-1-62143-2876 (hardcover)
978-1-62143-2968 (paperback)
978-1-62143-3057 (hosted ebook)

Library of Congress Control Number: 2015939657

Printed in the United States of America
Mankato, MN
July, 2015

CONTENTS

CHAPTER 1
ON THE SPOT

Carey Price stared down the ice. Peter Mueller began charging toward him. Mueller was 18. Price was 19. Both had been red hot. And both had their country's hopes on the line.

It was the 2007 World Junior Championships in Sweden. Price's Team Canada faced Mueller's Team USA. The winner would move on to the title game. And the teams were deadlocked. They had played a 10-minute overtime. Yet they were still tied. So it all came down to a shootout.

Price had faced Patrick Kane in the first round. Kane's tricky puck handling could fool even the best goalies. But not Price. Not on this day. He stayed on his skates. Kane had to skate wide. At the last

moment, Price dropped and spread his legs. Kane's shot bounced off Price's right skate.

Price faced Mueller for the first time in round two. Mueller flicked a shot past Price's glove. But after three rounds, the teams were tied 2–2. That meant sudden death. Teams could now reuse shooters. And after Canada missed, Team USA sent Kane

Price, *front centre*, and Team Canada celebrate winning the 2007 World Junior Championships.

back out. He could win it with a goal. But Price was ready. Kane tried to shoot between Price's legs. Price snapped them shut and held on to the puck.

QUICK STAT

Price had six wins and two shutouts in the World Junior Championships.

Jonathan Toews then scored for Canada. But Mueller answered with another glove-side goal. Both teams scored in round six, too. Then Toews scored his third shootout goal. That's when Price found himself again facing Mueller.

Team USA needed a goal to stay alive. Mueller collected the puck and skated toward Price. He made a move. Then he went glove-side again. This time Price was ready. He blocked the puck! Price usually looks calm and relaxed on the ice. After this save, he pumped his fist. Canada's players rushed onto the ice to celebrate.

Canada went on to beat Russia 4–2 in the final. It was the country's third straight World Juniors title. Price was named the tournament's best goaltender. He also won Most Valuable Player (MVP) honours. Montreal Canadiens fans were watching. They were ready for Price to bring his game to the National Hockey League (NHL).

World Junior Talent

The World Junior Championships is a major event each year. The players are age 20 or younger. Some will go on to become NHL stars. Many future stars played in the 2007 event. Team USA's Patrick Kane was the first pick in the 2007 NHL draft. Canada had many talented players, too. Among them were Cody Franson, Kris Letang, Brad Marchand, Marc Staal, and Jonathan Toews. Peter Mueller also played five seasons in the NHL.

CHAPTER 2
TAKING OFF

Carey Price was born on August 16, 1987. He grew up in Anahim Lake. That is a small town in northern British Columbia. Only 700 people lived there. The Corkscrew Creek ran behind the Price family house. Carey's dad, Jerry, shovelled it off in the winter. He taught Carey to skate when the boy was just three years old.

Every night, Carey and his dad would go skating. As Carey got older, he started taking shots. Then he decided to try playing goalie. Jerry had been a goalie, too. He made Carey's first mask. Carey liked playing there right away. He studied the best NHL goalies. Marty Turco and Martin Brodeur were two of his favourites. Carey also learned a lot from his dad.

Around age nine, Carey was ready to play on a team. That was a problem. Anahim Lake didn't have a team. The closest one was in Williams Lake, British Columbia. It was 320 kilometres away. That didn't stop the Prices. Carey and Jerry made the long trip three times each week. Soon the drive became too hard, though. Jerry had a new idea. He had a pilot's

Carey and his dad flew in a small four-seat airplane like this one.

QUICK STAT

Price had a 2.74 goals-against average (GAA) in his final season with Williams Lake in 2002–03.

license. So he bought a small airplane. After that, they flew to practices and games.

Their efforts began paying off. By his teens Carey had become one of the best young players in Canada. Junior hockey teams wanted Carey. He decided to play in the Western Hockey League. The Tri-City Americans picked him seventh overall in that league's draft. It was an exciting time for Carey. But it was also a time of change. The team was based far away in Kennewick, Washington. Carey was just 16 years old. He would have to leave his family, his friends, and even his home country. In addition, his new city was much bigger than Anahim Lake. He didn't let that stop him, though. Carey packed his bags and headed south.

Carey's Family

Jerry Price was a pretty good goalie in his day. The Philadelphia Flyers drafted him in 1978. But Jerry had some tough injuries. He never got out of the minor leagues. Carey's mother is Lynda. She is a member of Canada's First Nations. She was the former chief of the Ulkatcho First Nation. Carey also has one sister, Kayla. Arizona Coyotes captain Shane Doan is a cousin of Carey's.

CHAPTER 3

THROUGH JUNIORS

Carey was a quiet kid. Sometimes he felt out of place in his new home. Lucky for Carey, he had support. He lived with a host family. Dennis and Jill Williams helped Carey adjust to Washington. They took care of Carey. Their support helped him feel more at home.

Adjusting to his new team was easier. Carey began as the Tri-City Americans' backup goalie. The starter, Tyler Weiman,

Price plays in a top-prospects game in 2005.

was 19 years old. He was on his way to a pro career. Carey didn't let Tyler's talent bother him. He came to practice every day and worked hard on his skills. Before long, his coach noticed. Carey began playing more and more. By the playoffs, Carey was the starter.

Carey played three more seasons with the Americans. The team made the playoffs every year. Carey was especially good in his second year. He set records for shutouts and goals-against average in

2004–05. His talent was clear. But some people were unsure what to think of Carey. He didn't talk much. He always looked calm and relaxed. Some people thought this meant he was lazy. But really, the game just came easy to Carey.

The relaxed style worked for Carey. NHL teams agreed. The Montreal Canadiens picked him fifth in the 2005 NHL draft. Montreal already had a star goalie in José Théodore. But the team decided it couldn't pass on Carey.

Carey still needed more experience. So he stayed with Tri-City in 2005–06 and 2006–07. Then came his performance at the 2007 World Junior Championships. The Canadiens knew he was close.

Life off the Ice

Junior players are on the ice a lot. Carey enjoyed his time away from the rink, though. Dennis Williams taught Carey how to bow hunt. Dennis and Carey did target practice in the back yard. They shot arrows into a bale of hay. Carey also enjoyed lassoing. He used to practice while watching TV.

CHAPTER 4

THE NHL CALLS

P rice's junior career ended on a down note. The Tri-City Americans were knocked out of the 2007 playoffs early. But that opened a new opportunity for Price. One day later, he officially joined the Canadiens organization. They assigned him to their minor league team. So he headed to Hamilton, Ontario. The Hamilton Bulldogs' season was almost over. The Bulldogs started Price right away.

It was a good decision. Price played just two regular-season games. Then he led the Bulldogs to the league championship. He won 15 games and had a .936 save percentage. At 19, he was named playoffs MVP. The last teenage goalie to win that honour was Patrick Roy in 1985. Roy went on to

become a superstar for Montreal. Price followed that path a few months later.

Price made his NHL debut on October 10, 2007. He had 26 saves against the Pittsburgh Penguins. Montreal won 3–2. His strong play continued. Price was named to the NHL's All-Rookie Team that season. Price wasn't immediately a star, though.

Price gets in position to stop Vancouver Canucks forward David Booth in a 2012 game.

He spent some time in the minors that year. He continued to share goalie duties in Montreal over his first few seasons. Some fans expected him to be better. Montreal has high standards for goalies. Some of the best of all time have played there. It took Price a while to prove he belonged.

"You learn a lot of lessons playing in a place like this," he said. "You face a lot more pressure than on other teams."

The Canadiens believed in Price. Before the 2010–11 season, they signed him to a new contract. They also named him their starter. Price answered with his best NHL season. He led the league in wins. He also allowed the fewest goals per game of his career. Price played really well in the playoffs. But the Canadiens lost in the first round. Before the 2012–13 season, Price signed a new six-year contract. He was going to be Montreal's goalie for a long time.

Historic Habs

The Canadiens have a rich history. No team comes close to the team's 24 Stanley Cup wins. Many great goalies have played for the Canadiens. Among them were Jacques Plante, Ken Dryden, and Patrick Roy. All three are in the Hockey Hall of Fame. The Canadiens' locker room is filled with pictures of great players. Price's locker is right underneath Roy's picture.

CHAPTER 5
SHINING IN SOCHI

Expectations were high for Team Canada going into the 2014 Olympics. There was also a great debate. Who should be the starting goalie? Roberto Luongo had led Canada to the 2010 gold medal. But many believed Price was better in 2014.

The Winter Games were in Sochi, Russia. Price's parents went to watch him play. Coach Mike Babcock picked Price to start Canada's first game. He stopped 19 shots in a 3–1 win over Norway. But Luongo started the next game. Canada won that one, too. Then Price got the call again. He made 14 saves as Canada beat Finland 2–1 in overtime.

Babcock had seen enough. He named Price the starter for the quarter-finals against Latvia. And Price came through again. Behind a strong defence, Price faced just 16 shots. He saved 15. That was enough for a 2–1 win. The biggest test was coming up, though.

Canada faced Team USA in the semi-finals. It was just like the 2007 World Junior Championships. Both teams were really good. Neither had lost yet. But only one could move on to the championship game.

21

Both teams came out hard. The Americans pressured Price more than the other teams. But Price stayed calm. He kept stopping shots. There was a problem, though. Team USA goalie Jonathan Quick was hot, too. Jamie Benn finally scored for Canada in the second period. Price did the rest. He stopped all 31 shots he faced. Canada won 1–0.

The gold-medal game against Sweden was next. Sweden also had not yet lost in the Olympics. But like Team USA, Sweden could not get a puck past Price. He stopped 24 shots for his second straight shutout. Canada won 3–0. It was the country's ninth Olympic gold medal.

Price was named the Olympics' best goalie.

Wild Wedding

Price met Angela Webber when playing for the Tri-City Americans. She was from Kennewick, Washington. They began dating. In 2013 they got married in Kennewick. The wedding came during a very busy week for Price. He had to leave the very next day to practice with Team Canada for the Olympics.

His numbers were excellent. He played in five games. Opponents scored just three goals against him. And he was at his best in the biggest games. Price could not have done it alone. He made sure to recognize his teammates for playing great defence.

CHAPTER 6

COOL CANADIEN

Price was already an NHL star. After the Olympics, he was even more famous. But Price had little time to celebrate. The Canadiens' season picked up just a few days later. And they were having a great season. They went on to have their best record since 2007–08.

The hot streak continued in the playoffs. Montreal swept the Tampa Bay Lightning. Then it beat the Boston Bruins in seven games. That put the Canadiens in the conference finals. They were just one series shy of the Stanley Cup Final. Only the New York Rangers stood in the way.

Price makes a save against the rival Boston Bruins in the 2014 NHL playoffs.

Fans were excited for the series. But things quickly soured. Rangers forward Chris Kreider ran into Price in the second period of Game 1. Price tried to keep playing. It didn't end well. The Rangers scored two goals. At the intermission, Price left the game with a knee injury. That was the end of his season. The Rangers went on to win in six games.

Price makes a save during a 2015 game against the Dallas Stars.

QUICK STAT

Price's 44 wins, 1.96 GAA, and .933 save percentage led the NHL in 2014–15.

Price came back to record career highs in wins, save percentage, GAA, and shutouts in 2014–15. His steady play and puck-handling ability helped his teammates. They knew Price didn't often panic or make mistakes. That allowed them to play more aggressively.

With Price in net, the Canadiens had the second-best record in the league. Price continued to thrive in the playoffs. But the Tampa Bay Lightning eliminated Montreal in the second round.

After the playoffs, Price was rewarded for his great season by winning two prestigious awards. He received the Vezina Trophy, given to the NHL's best goalie each season. He also earned the Hart Trophy, given to the NHL's MVP. There was little doubt that he was now among the game's elite players. And Canadiens fans could be sure they had found another great goalie.

Community Leader

Carey and Angela Price do a lot to help others. The Canadiens awarded him the Jean Beliveau Trophy in 2013–14. It goes each year to a Canadiens player who is a leader in his community. Price is active in many causes. He is very passionate about helping students. He encourages them to stay in school by giving free tickets to every Canadiens game for students with good attendance.

Timeline

1. **Vancouver, British Columbia 1987**
   Carey Price is born on August 16.

2. **Anahim Lake, British Columbia 1987–96**
   Price spends the early part of his life here.

3. **Williams Lake, British Columbia 1996–2003**
   Price plays hockey for the Williams Lake Timberwolves because there is no team in Anahim Lake.

4. **Kennewick, Washington 2002–07**
   Price joins the Tri-City Americans, a junior hockey team. As the primary starting goalie, he leads the team to the playoffs in 2004–05, 2005–06, and 2006–07.

5. **Hamilton, Ontario 2007–08**
   After signing with the Canadiens, Price plays with their minor league team, the American Hockey League's Hamilton Bulldogs. He leads them to the 2007 championship.

6. **Montreal, Quebec 2007–**
   Price joins the Canadiens. He becomes the team's primary starting goalie in 2010–11.

7. **Pittsburgh, Pennsylvania 2007**
   Price makes his NHL debut on October 10 and helps the Canadiens beat the Penguins 3–2.

8. **Tampa, Florida 2015**
   Despite a strong effort from Price, the Canadiens fall in six games to the Tampa Bay Lightning in the Eastern Conference semi-finals.

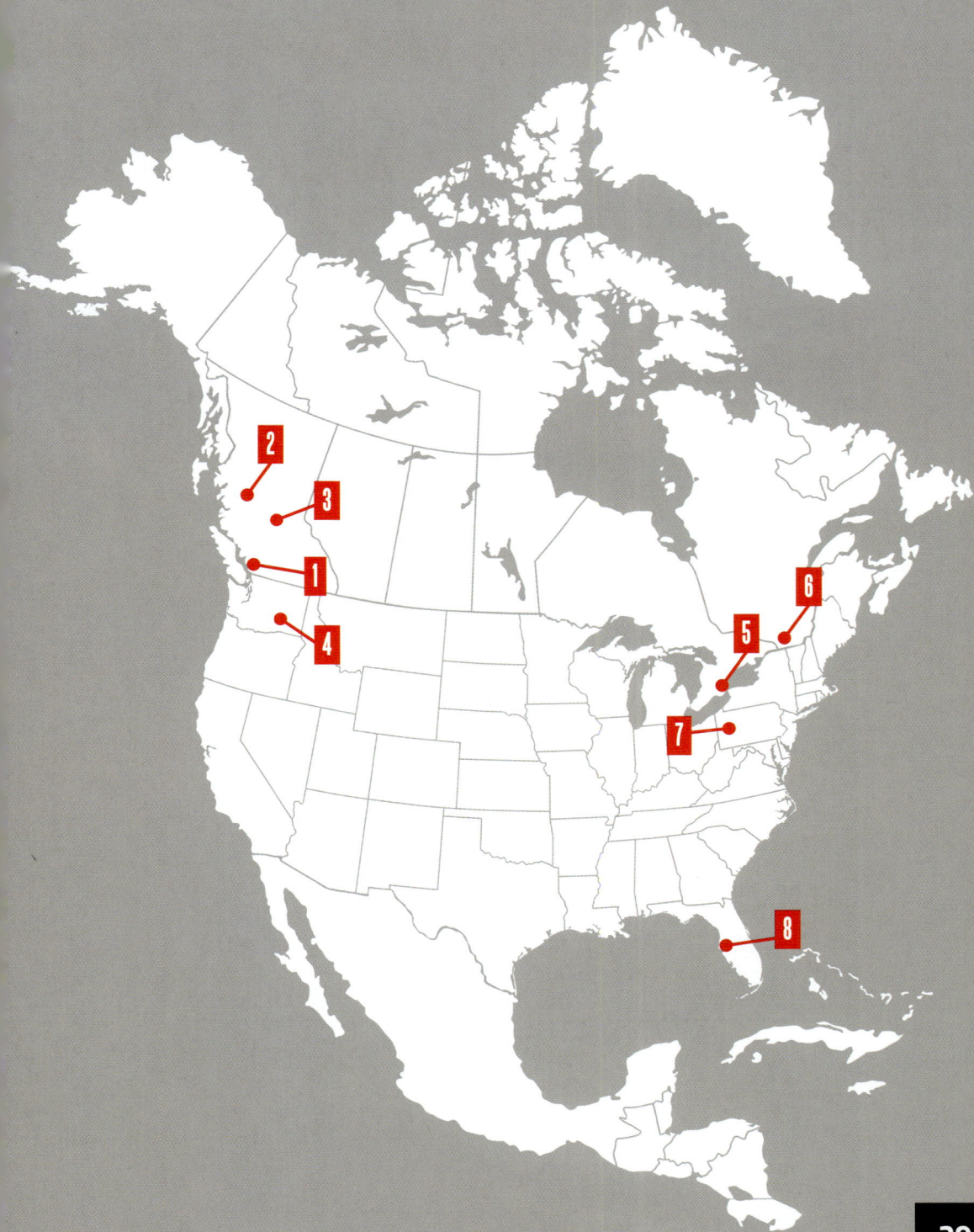

Carey Price at a Glance

FULL NAME: Carey Price

BIRTH DATE: August 16, 1987

BIRTHPLACE: Anahim Lake, British Columbia

JUNIOR TEAM: Tri-City Americans (2002–07)

TEAM CANADA:
- Olympic Games: 2014 (first place)
- World Junior Championships: 2006–07 (first)
- Honours: Best Goalkeeper Award 2014 Olympics

NHL:
- Team: Montreal Canadiens (2007–)
- Honours: Hart Memorial Trophy (MVP) 2014–15; Vezina Trophy (Best Goalie) 2014–15; First-Team All-Star 2014–15; four All-Star Games

NHL BEST SEASONS:

WINS	GOALS-AGAINST AVERAGE	SAVE PERCENTAGE
44 (2014–15)	1.96 (2014–15)	.933 (2014–15)

Glossary

CONTRACT: a legal agreement between two parties

DRAFT: a system in which teams in a league can select incoming players

ROOKIE: a first-year player

SHOOTOUT: a way of deciding a winner when the score remains tied after overtime; both teams select players to take penalty shots until there is a winner

SHUTOUT: when a goalie allows no goals in a game

SUDDEN DEATH: one-off rounds of a shootout; these take place if the shootout is tied after three rounds

For More Information

BOOKS

Peters, Chris. *Great Moments in Olympic Ice Hockey*. Minneapolis, MN: Abdo Publishing Co., 2015.

Stewart, Mark. *The Montreal Canadiens*. Chicago, IL: Norwood House Press, 2014.

WEB SITES

Hockey Canada
www.hockeycanada.ca

Montreal Canadiens
canadiens.nhl.com

Index

About the Author

Todd Kortemeier is a writer and journalist from Minneapolis. He is a graduate of the University of Minnesota's School of Journalism & Mass Communication.